I love reading

KU-790-237

Bug Watch

by Monica Hughes

Editorial consultant: Mitch Cronick

ticktock

Copyright © **ticktock Entertainment Ltd 2006**
First published in Great Britain in 2006 by **ticktock Media Ltd.,**
Unit 2, Orchard Business Centre, North Farm Road, Tunbridge Wells, Kent TN2 3XF

We would like to thank: Shirley Bickler and Suzanne Baker

ISBN 1 86007 972 5 pbk
Printed in China

Picture credits
t=top, b=bottom, c=centre, l-left, r=right, OFC= outside front cover
Science Photo Library: 7. Shutterstock: 8-9, 10, 16-17, 18-21.
Superstock: 11, 17tr. ticktock photography: 4, 5, 6, 12-13.

Every effort has been made to trace the copyright holders, and we apologise in advance for any unintentional omissions. We would be pleased to insert the appropriate acknowledgements in any subsequent edition of this publication.

A CIP catalogue record for this book is available from the British Library. All rights reserved. No part of this publication may be reproduced, copied, stored in a retrieval system or transmitted in any form or by any means electronic, mechanical, photocopying, recording or otherwise without prior written permission of the copyright owner.

CONTENTS

Insects

The bugs in this book are insects.

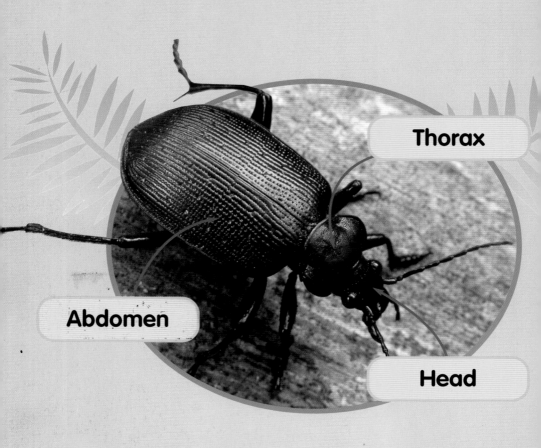

Thorax

Abdomen

Head

4

All insects have a body with three parts.

Most insects have two antennae...

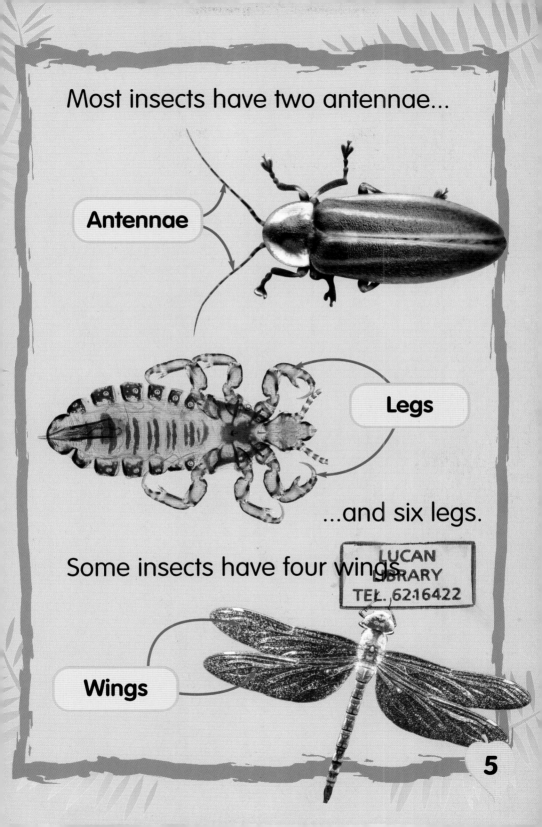

Antennae

Legs

...and six legs.

Some insects have four wings.

LUCAN LIBRARY
TEL. 6216422

Wings

5

Ladybirds

There are many different kinds of ladybird.

Head

Thorax

Abdomen

Most ladybirds are red with black spots.

Some ladybirds are yellow.

6

Ladybirds live in gardens and parks.

Aphids

Ladybirds eat small
bugs called aphids.

Ants

Ants eat other insects.

Ants also eat the honeydew that aphids make.

Honeydew is runny and sweet.

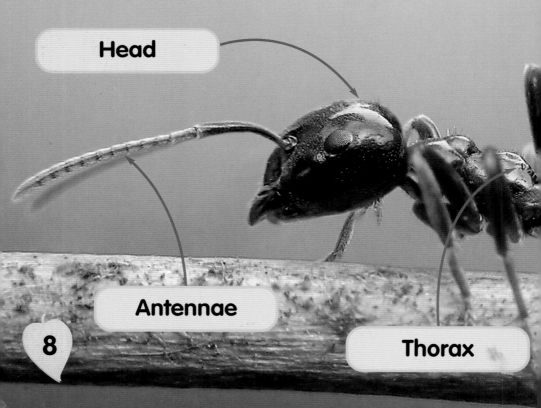

Head

Antennae

Thorax

This is an ants' nest.

Ants live in big groups.

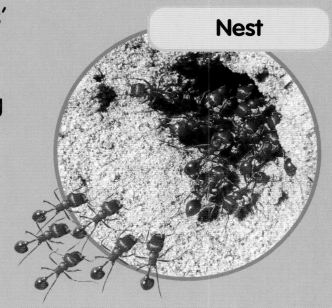

Nest

Abdomen

Dragonflies

There are many different kinds of dragonfly.

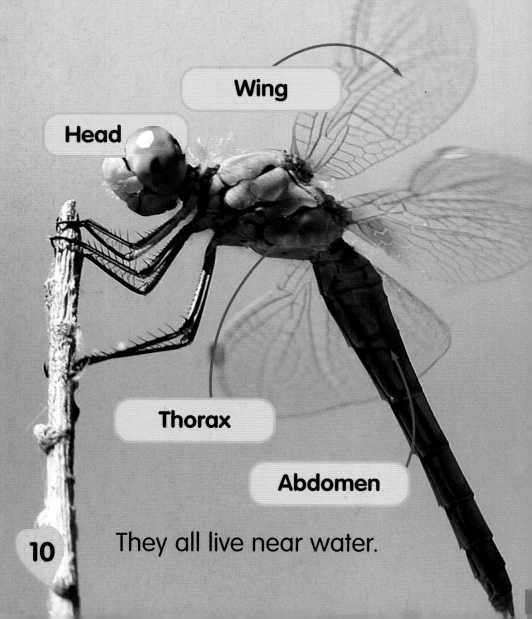

Wing

Head

Thorax

Abdomen

They all live near water.

An adult dragonfly has a long body.

It has four wings.

Dragonflies eat flying insects.

Butterflies

There are many different kinds of butterfly.

Tongue

They feed on the nectar from flowers.

Nectar is runny and sweet.

12

Antennae

Some butterflies only live for one day.

Head lice

Head lice live on clean hair.

They feed on human blood.

Head lice do not have wings.

They cannot fly.

They crawl from head to head.

Abdomen

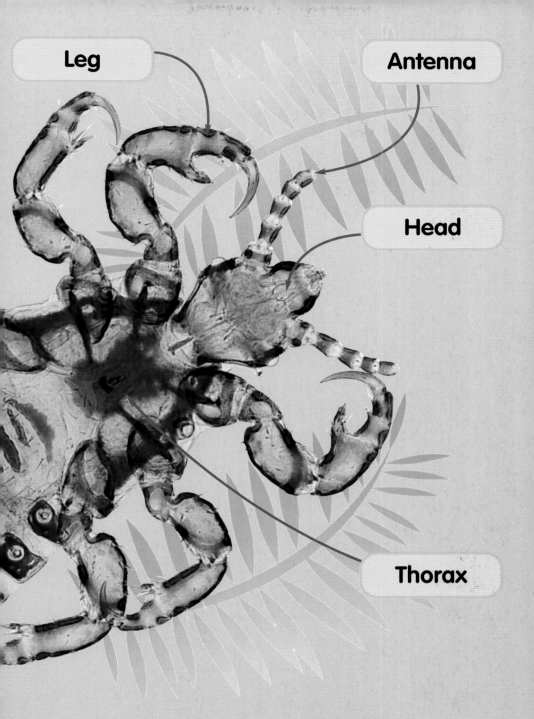

Leg

Antenna

Head

Thorax

15

Aphids

Aphids live on plants and trees.

They eat the sap in the leaves.

Sap is a runny liquid.

Aphids

Aphids make honeydew.

Ants eat the honeydew.

Ladybirds eat aphids.

Ant

Life cycles

All insects start life as eggs.

They change as they get older.

Some change from an egg to a nymph.

Then they change from a nymph to an adult

Dragonfly

Aphid

Head louse

An aphid, a head louse and a
dragonfly change in this way.

Dragonfly life cycle

Eggs

Nymph

Adult

More life cycles

Some insects change three times.

They begin life as an egg.

Then they change to a larva, then to
a pupa.

Then they change from a pupa to an adult.

Butterfly

Ladybird

Ant

Ants, ladybirds and butterflies change
in this way.

Caterpillar

A butterfly larva is called a caterpillar.

Butterfly life cycle

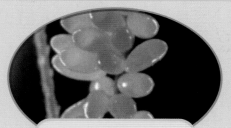

Eggs

Larva

Pupa

Adult

Talking about insects

What do all insects have?

- **A three part body**
- **Legs, wings and antennae**

How many times do these insects change?

- **Ants**
- **Ladybirds**
- **Butterflies**

Which of these insects eat nectar?

- **Head louse**
- **Ant**

- **Butterfly**

Where do
aphids live?

- **In a nest**

- **Underwater**

- **On plants and trees**

Which insect would you like to be?
Why?

LUCAN
LIBRARY
TEL. 62·16422

Activities

What did you think of this book?

 Brilliant   **Good**   **OK**

Which page did you like best? Why?

• • • • • • • • • • • • • • •

Put these life cycle words in the right order.

nymph • adult • egg

• • • • • • • • • • • • • •

Invent an insect! Draw a big picture and label it. Use these words:

wings • head • thorax • abdomen

• • • • • • • • • • • • • •

Who is the author of this book?
Have you read *Scary Snakes* by the same author?